poets + jugglers

We Not Kids
No more

ALSO BY DOMINIC ALBANESE

poets + jugglers

poems by
Dominic Albanese

Poetic Justice Books
Port St. Lucie, Florida

book design and layout: SpiNDec, Port Saint Lucie, FL
cover design: Kris Haggblom, PSL, FL
Trickster with a Monkey Wrench ©2019 Alicia Young

Published by Poetic Justice Books
Port Saint Lucie, Florida
www.poeticjusticebooks.com

ISBN: 978-1-950433-21-6

FIRST EDITION
10 9 8 7 6 5 4 3 2 1

MARY LORRAINE METCALF...
forgive me mother
I did not ever mean
to speak so harsh to or about you

TRICKSTER WITH A MONKEY WRENCH

Dominic Albanese writes like a Benedictine monk who kicked a cocaine addiction and picked up a poetry habit. His writing serves to remind us that there's never been a war since the Iron Age that wasn't fought by children. His poignant, incendiary poetry blasts from the page in short bursts of gunfire wordplay. Albanese is a rough and tumble, hyperactive, second-generation American of Irish and Italian immigrants. He waxes fantastic about the sirens of Coney Island, the jungles of Vietnam, and the sub cultures of 20th Century San Francisco. Rife with the imagery of love, loss, religion, and drugs, you will smell his mother's alcoholic breath, you will see the callouses on his father's hands, you will feel the bullets and Bay breezes rocketing past your head as you ride along with this firecracker. However, don't let this fucker fool you, he's a poet, which means he will break your heart, and leave you on Mission Boulevard weeping. He's a trickster with a monkey wrench for a pen. He leaves his words bolted together, covered in grease, but I'll be damned if it doesn't get your engine purring.

— *Alicia Young; Cincinnati,OH 2019*

poets
+
jugglers

NOT SURE

or able to pin
point exactly
where the Jabberwocky
meets Beowulf ... or ... lives of quiet desperation
intersect
but
it does seem to me
life banana peels n orange juice
have conspired
in
either ... fact fantasy or
drop dead reality

IF I

try to wrap my
mind around
inequality
parity
or justice
I get
a
really
bad
headache

RIP

fuck that
I will
howl from
my grave
scorn n lash out
at
a brainless line of
stupid
waiting for
daddy to come
save them
or some new Mom with
a
big bank roll

NOTHING LEFT

but some
faded flower petals
a distant linger
for "adult conversations"
dodging intimacy
like punches
get what was needed wanted tops adore
n
run in a hail of angry slather
that
can
never
be put back
in the can
it never should
have been let out of
person place yet
to
be
"OVER"

ANOTHER POEM

after burn of
cherry blossoms
passing on a train
sent shivers up
my brain
kicked in a rhyme gland
again

IN SPITE

of places I have
been
things I have done
experiences both regret or enjoy
big parts of me
are
still
a sad little boy

TRIBUTE TO JOYCE ... in make us all keep guessing ... as current events are pressing ... have a coup of country or a cup of java ... let yr mind wander ... in some urban forest of glass concrete n steel ... keep that gossamer blouse beauty out of eye range in some grassy glen for when ... days become to hard to bear ... with information on a tear ... with that once or twice a lifetime ... it all seems to "come together" ... as Molly n that portrait artist or deep pool of HCE n another novel ... more of an code like tomb raiders try n fail to decipher ... have tea ... be you be me ... in an insane time ... with out any anger ... or fear ... what the fuck is going on here ... to my own land ... yes even if I only own a very small part of it ... or not a bit as the tax rolls forever price me out of home n office ... let me be ... let it be ... n yes ... between the lyrics of bands ... the lay on of hands ... all over middle earth ... from Amok to Hong Kong ... from Delaware to Patagonia ... mystery fiction ... high art ... low brow ... pulp ... n all the comic books ever wound up in land fill ... please take a moment to be silent ... then scream ... as hat rack ... hard dicks n warm vagina are still matters of speculation ... expectation ... sex as a sport or sex as death ... in transit ... all manner of false flag propaganda infects us ... we can all ... sit quiet with a book an go boldly where some have gone before but never with our eyes n brain ... like indeed "strangers on a train" ... who are you what is your name ... why do you have that smile was it from yesterday ... or hope about tomorrow

THAT OLD MAN

who had a voice
like thunder
n hands
big as catchers mitts
who could tell ya
where + when
bout anything ... from
baseball to Catherine of Aragon
sitting drinking iced coffee ... doing a
cross word puzzle ... humming a show tune
looking out the window
on never

AFTER SCROLL BLUES

noise ... lies ... human
barbarity
got a cup ... went deck sit
first a flicker chases a cardinal
then pair of yellow butterflies
do
a wing mate dance
half a cup
later
everything
yes my baby girl
everything
is gonna
be all right

FORGIVE ME

I was young
impressionable
I did not even know
of DAU TRANH strategy
or
real liberation
I do now
too late
I like my country
made a lot of mistakes
forgive me
kiem thao I have
cried enough

or ... a mandatory obey vaccine
dark to dawn curfew
rationed gas
rationed food
as if
Mr. Orwell's book
was
an
instruction manual
or ... small groups of
haters
with file sharpened teeth
n
loads of guns ... ammo ... n beer
holy history books n history book
writers
you ain't seen nothing like blue berry yogurt

TITLE ON BOTTOM

BAFFLED

between politics
of murder
(we have started 4 wars ya know)
innocence is a
passing thought
now
yr fucking dead so
if ya did it or not
ya wont do it again
hop hop little bunny
fore
you get blamed
my heart is in a thousand bits
this morning
life ... only life
rest of it
is underground rotting away
on an almost perfect
day

A PAEAN

to the historically uninformed
as
if Elvis in 57 John Paul George n Ringo in 65
meant significant dents
in world affairs
they did how ever like Franky boy earlier
cause major heart throb intense *feelings*
no
it was only 1924
last date recorded of Caliphate
power
seems like entertainment ... sports ... fashion
endless new products must have consumer
goods apparel toys cars boats
let me show you a gigabyte hermaphrodite break
thru
in
tents along date tree oasis
hide outs old camel trails
call wink promise palaver entice
a return to some pure religious fanaticism
dreaming of turbans engraved swords
a moral sickness infected humans
try to re-create I bin El Sal a din come calling
mean while remote controls are frenzy program
to
not miss a minute of NFL action ...
stump bump silly me ... Allah + Jesus
play cards ... wondering where
they fucked up ...

THAT FOUND

moment
tis a poem born of
adjusting digesting
cover ears to not let
a word sound escape
that best taken slow
attention to detail
with a pause for ginger ale
interrupted flow
no where to go
but
one more line
about her

"if you have trouble walking just look at your feet"
A bit of either over heard or read ... conversations
... in case of fire use nearest exit ... that out ward
bound roll over baby I have a yank crank game to
play with you ... in mid sentence ... grated window
blind reflections shimmer ... shake ... counting hours
as minutes days as weeks ... it is all part of a born
awake ... only to cry ... then die ... in the middle of
this afternoon's nap came a voice ... singing ... birds
eat bugs n bugs eat bugs ... cooked up we eat em
all ... now having had these high surf swim days ...
coated with salt walking with a bit of sway ... look-
ing down at feet ... all of creations slides away ...
In a small Church in Sicily ... one candle burns for
St Lucia that blind woman who fed poor people
... along Ave B in New York ... a once great poet ...
drinks cheap wine ... speaks to Bob Kaufman's ghost
... in language only they speak ... or understand

PREHISTORIC VIRUS

o piddle paddle
fiddle faddle
now I gotta worry
bout
some shit been buried in
polar ice since ... Og ... n Nog ... had a fight
over who ate the last
Mastodon bone' pesticide herbicide
un burned hydro carbons
PPB DDT DEA CIA FBI
NSA ... padded bras ... germs in spas
calafragic etiologic scatology ... poop inspection
traumatic acid trips n
loose wheel bearings

it indeed is bed time

ANTOMORPHAFIZE

ya got *zombies?* do ya
in cheap ass make up stumble around
an look *stupid*
well let me tell you bout *horror*
ok
big fire ant mounds
(that movie bout shrinking people?)
OK
I am about a 1/64 inch long
n down in the belly of the beasts I go
OK ... rappel down (cloak device enabled)
n
here in detail ... first there is the queen's chamber
OK
n 900 bare naked motherfucking bad ass storm
troopers guard her with razor sharp swords
pantry part ... a host of dead bugs snakes bits
of road kill ... assorted chunks of who da fk knows
all masticated n turned into mush to feed
THE MATERNITY WARD ... a billion little hungry
future piss ant stinging foraging soon to be
bite yr ass n laugh gangs develop murder skills
climb back up my monofilament escape rope
poof return to *full size* and sit deck side
contemplating a small tactical assault squad
of tiny special ops guys to go and
shoot dem fucks with tiny little guns
an den hang dere asses on the fender
n come home here to a ticker tape parade

IMPOSSIBLE

to either know
how or why
a mention of location
can trigger "events ... time ... places gone"
Philadelphia ... I bet I have not thought
of that city since Rocky came out
but
Spring semester at Philly College of Art 67
I was an artist model and worked nights
at the ZU ZU room as a bouncer
My Brother made book bar side ... at
The Parker Hotel
I was in love with a really wild gal
(whose father had been blackballed by McCarthy)
any way she ran off
with my motorcycle an another guy
to Mexico ... and I went n stole another bike
n went back to New York
where I met my Daughter's Mother
whose father was also given
the McCarthy "are you now or have you ever been
a member of the communist party?"
he was ... and had to play piano in the Symphony
till he could teach again ... many years later
any way
how location ... or mention of
can find a mural painted on brain cells
out of "the still dark past"
is why I am
so glad

I have lived long enough
to have
lived
enough
to write it down now

INCANTATIONS REDUX

"a moments sunlight fading in the grass"
lot of years ago
concepts ideas ... songs n pleading
for
meaning
as
now
scroll post store in "activity log"
a
perhaps record
of
Kilroy was here
in
data ... beep ... xo,xo ... likes n comments
does
life depend on emoji
or on
sunlight fading in
the grass

EMPIRICAL ELASTIC

OK ... fuck Gibbons
holy Roman empire my
toe nail fungus
among us
today
is a band of rubber bullshit
called "American Interests Abroad"
that
bout to snap ... crackle ... pop
n not rice krispies
nope ... unless your kids
can eat
un-exploded munitions
or surplus military hardware
is the new designer rage
ya bout to read a book
that
has no last page
just scrolled cross it in italics
the end

AND NOW

brought to you
by
your unending need to
burn gas
going no pace fast
oil is spewed into
ROLL ON COLUMBIA
a river
already taxed to the max

by dams n pollution
a host of
sea lions ... a gaggle of shitting geese
hog lines ... pristine lawns ... full of round up
n other corporate poison
cause
ya gotta keep up
appearances
as below surface sturgeon
who
are old very very old
wag chin whiskers ... n smell
crude oil death

CONTRAST

of cloud cover
when
I seek light in shadows
of what once was
as
facing up to
all but love now
is indeed
a trick of light
day to night
adjust your screen
for better clarity
or
stand by
this just in
we lost
they win

ONLY GUY I KNOW

who really knew
Ali
as a friend
you went to Africa
with the CHAMP
may
he remember you
may he get to
tease Joe Frazier
n
be all limber an funny
again
as serious as he
was
a true hero
of truth ... who did
tell it like it is
over n over again

{*Big Black - world's best hand drummer*}

DID

they tell
the truth
bout JFK
9/11
why Jack fell down
n
Jill stayed dry?
did they?
an
ya want da FBI
to indict a dragon lady
you
really watch too
much smelly vision
n
read too many
meme
A Government that is
a
carnival n we are
marks
ba ba ba ... did ya vote? did ya?
here try again
yr Kewpie doll is on a boat
from China
be here in November

POETS + JUGGLERS

both of em
throw stuff
up
trying to catch
it
as
it falls

LIBERATION

free from
dragons ... dark hearts
demented souls who
seek to drag another
into shame guilt depression
as
if food ... could do more than
feed you
empty hearts are never stated
only
left looking at passer by
in
either sorrow or jealousy ... Ima take my
self for
a walk n smile at everybody
my liberation is clear now
you are I am
"an we are all together" ... TO GET HER.how that
word
is spell ... like a full on battalion of airborne troopers
saving me from not
getting my self

ORLANDO

is a tragic reminder
of how
death is not part of
life liberty n the pursuit of happiness
no ... and just as a dire warning
this is not local ... national it is global
if China
bulldozes the monastic home
of thousands of monk n nuns
who spend a life time praying
an in the world not of the world
as monastics do
wait ... money? freedom? TV n cell phones
or other material goals
wait
once the truly prayerful go
only thing left is hate n violence
as we wonder why

ABLE

to start over
omuphtafaddlebut
I was so blue
this morning
I could a been a smurf
nope
long nap ... ooooooo
what nice dreams
as if some silent movie
queen
came to me n whisper
fear not fat boy
only way ya really know what
joy
is
requires a plunge sponge to
morose or tooth decay
got
up
jumped in da pool
swam my sad ass long face
ass
to a
brand new day

CARE NOT

me
to be
taken serious
by
the serious
nope
dig it daddy o
joined up wit
da
delirious years ago
wags nags critics n
"of high born order"
can
kiss my grubby stubby
ass

DELETED

a poem
there is enough
snark
all over ... l need not add
an no matter the motivation
of the sit in in congress
some action
beats the living fuck
outta none at all
but ... death by gun
death by drone
the dead
all
die
alone

GONNA

put down
my
mouse n tab
gonna let ...
my feed go by
ain't gonna share no
more
pictures of ghosts
or news items toast
I got fooled again
"share now ... public ... yr time line
a friends time line ... in a group in a message"
fuck all that
Mr. Rodgers was a Navy seal
some 9 year old
shot mom + dad
over wi-fi
mother scrunchy
my knickers in a bunchy
not since I found out Midnight the cat
was not real
now thru painful and deep searching
find out
every thing on line
is
not "true" whoa ... bat man
too

ONE DAY

after mold
decay
worms n time
have
reduced you
rendered you
bare bones
83 years from now
some
body in some
"research center"
is gonna see a picture
of your lunch
on some dvd type recorded
trail of social inter change now
face book like old silent movies
are now ... quaint n sort of either
tribal tonal myths memories music
or indeed History and really
wonder???? what the fuck
were they thinking

VINDICATED

yup
indeed
necktie ... wearing
double talking
feet shuffling
walk backwards
politicians
are way
way way
more
fulla shit
en
I am

NEWS FLASH

some of the current
"Christian" churches
have more in common
with ISIS en ya wanna hear
bigots … whiners … blame game
experts
who
have never really understood
true religion
"aiding widows n orphans in need"
how ever
since in the last 60 some
years we … yes US … the good ole USA
have made more
widows n orphans
en we aid
go back to that part
about "so have you done to the least of me
you have done unto me"
or
that bizz bout casting the first stone
all of it
line em up
mow em down
after all dead people don't need
money

CLEAR MINDED

a couple hours
on
a hidden lake
(small but fulla bass)
fully awake
looking back
I made a major mistake
that now
is re-verb ... conserve ... truth
simple
all most with out exception
every problem I ever had
(I created ... caused ... escaped or suffered for)
I have no fucking idea
what it is to be black in America
my skin color comes with a pass
in no way do
I agree w/ the fools ... I can surely be
one
when I open my yap
fulla swag n pap ... bout shit
I have no bizz to
so
I hereby ... make amends ... and spread a feather
pillow
in the wind
each collected feather
a tear ... for what I said
I most never should have

FUCK IT

snopes? fact check? research?
see the title
I like fake news way
better

FUCK FAUST

we are living
a deal w/ old ned
from artists to politicians
who
indeed sell them self
to
money + power
as if
food an water
or just clean air
are
only for those who
already have more
material wealth
needed by any one
just watch
from running for office
to selling
worth less critically acclaimed
fifty shades of shit
is
really the mark of
an
evolved social order

O SURE

they said
when I tried to complain
explain
this ... "lemming smart phone cliff jumping"
yup
I did
an was called ... lets see
a dinosaur
a relic
a stubborn old fuck
n an impede to social progress
of what I was called ... to fit here any way
now
ya gotta have a smart phone
to either
play poke yr eye out go
or
collect yr welfare check
sign up for the best deal
on
condoms to rocket trips
yup
and busy as 19 beavers
a cub bear trying to fornicate a foot ball
Mr. ... NSA an all his merry band of
alphabet bros
are in yr bizznezz
under yr skirt n up yr nose

FLOP

outta bed
coffee n wash my head
peruse da news
n make buzz buzz noise
(party to warn da world I am awake)
then
see some really juicy shit
on meme ... pee me ... but
I made my self a promise
fuck em
let da fight go on
reels to fix ... hot pix n romance
default zone ... bubble bubble
me only toil
me cause no trouble

NEWS

sports ... weather
24/7 ... all day all night
propaganda
inter spaced with
analyze prioritize comment
lie boldly looking right at the camera
with dewy eyes
in fact ... just in case ya did not know
is all really
a vast capitalist plot
to sell ya
repair replace adjust
yr toe nail fungus
n
yr limp penis ... throw
in some 9000 dollar cure
for ugly ... ya got the picture
of
today's information age

ESCAPE CLAUSE

X772209
as in
we have done such
a poor job
of caring for this planet ... (as a species a culture n
inhabitants)
some gang of both
science miners *faux star trek wanna be*
is spending trailer truck loads
of money to
find ... OK
methane lakes ... frozen relics of water
"canyons measureless to man"-----(could not help that)
or some new trailer park condo bunker warren hobbit hole
to
park their rich asses in when this
rock wither either explodes
sinks ... dribbles away melted like
a grand ice cream cone *the creator*
put us on
Buck Rodgers ... Capetian Zemo ... Ming the mercy
less
or a host of ... PK Dick ... William Gibson ... Walt
Disney
or HG Wells ... could be a part
but not really ... now the *punch line*
OK
I am offering stock options for

mineral metal massive deposits
of mother fletchers mozzzzarelllla cheese
and a free membership in
"lets find Alice Kramden fan club"
web address n pay pal sight
soon

OVER HEARD CAFE

chatter
he is cute but really fucking dumb
she had that same shirt on yesterday
one more word outta you not one more
some ass hole just farted
daily bits of
it
and I have really poor hearing
I have to walk by *slowly but looking at my phone*
that is the new *trade craft* your
phone
makes you invisible

SARTORIAL JEALOUSY

at long last
over
in that now I see
was
in deed a long agony
of
army/navy lasts
while smug preppies had
bass weguns
polyester corduroy vs
cotton + wool
now
(a serious revelation of how not good enough follows you)
flip flops old t-shirt n baggy shorts
if ya don't like me
just leave me alone

HAVING

spent 30 years
searching for
a daily reprieve ... based on spiritual condition
from
violence ... neon ... alley ways of desperation
(just about as long as since I punched someone)
I
had to really giggle at myself
getting up set
on cyber space
from words ... with no face
only some
parts of ... reflected in remarks
nerve ends bout 90% healed
under current ... tingle in background synapse
of
what used to get me
arrested on a regular basis
no
more ... no today ... not tomorrow
if
tomorrow indeed comes

THE AGES

of people
doing the dirt nap
have
me sit here
calculate capitulate copulate
my
windows ... wash em?
or see years pass
layers of salt air n dust
that
by this numerical algorithm
actuarial life expectancy
table of elements
well ... never mind ... but
push my old ass to 80
seems reasonable
but
"watch both ways"
less
ya
get
hit
by
a
truck full of flowers
or manure
and
wind up
kaput

U ARE WHAT

ya eat
so given a large
percentage of electric shopping cart
mountains of processed chemical left
over
side tracked
pesticide herbicide *patra n matra cide*
is
served up daily at smile face
balloons "save now die later"
portions of
our entire nature nation
are drowning in sugar bomb soda
n
the other bunch
exist on nicotine caffeine acid rain
n
what ever floats drifts or just falls outta
da sky
from Chernobyl or Fukushima
woop de fucking dooo

I GUESS

all this moral indignant
fist pumping
means not much
ignoring facts
WW2 did not last 9 years
5 of real combat ... lets piss on Yalta n then
money drunk weapons makers
saw gold where we saw blood
n
after Korea ... a minor skirmish
except to those who died there
Cold War went on 60 or more
to Vietnam and revise that shit all ya want
first American to die was a CIA guy in 56
then that horror went on till 75
Afghanistan + Iraq ===== see coup in 53
in Iran ... count the cards
buddy ... hold em or fold em
profit just went up n up
oil ... land ... gold ... pallets full of worthless
paper money
cause yr tax money paid for all them bullets
(mine too) ... and Central + South America.well shit
that has gone on since Cortez+Pizzaro ... not to
mention
Dr Henry Strangelove his merry gang of neo-cons
"all we are saying is give peace a chance"
yea John Lennon ... is dead
so
is Abe Lincoln ... not even to mention Mike Brown
or S. Bland ... nope ... yr money or yr life
what a stupid question

MY LIFE

wind less ... deck side
coffee n chapters
words
simple switches ... necro from neuro
a tale of post collapse plastic circuits
leading back falling over
advertising slogans *dura lux leather*
as
tomato plants could be hard wired
to
produce fruit in domed sanitized surfaces
coated to protect from
radio isotopes malware hidden tiny
transistors ... yearning for long gone
days
with a flashlight read under covers
n
Little Anthony singing bout
tears on my pillow

RITUALIZED INDOCTRINATION

huddled over coffee
n the new york times
or ... hearing a drone fog horn
voice of some pundit ... telling
you either all the fits or balanced and fair
is
akin
to reaching in a alligator pond to get
yr smart phone back ... See Capt. Hook n clock belly
ya will know what I mean
outrage ... stewing ... the style sections
makes a crack bout *sex n the thinking gal*
(S Brooks are you seeing this?)
and advertisement for a 800 dollar espresso maker
posed by a tennis player
the fuck ... the absolute fuck ... as
Syria's despot says he will re-build what
he has bombed
n ... yr watching the NFL? are ya?
hopalong cassidy ... n Sgt Joe Friday
are
part of this ... I just don't know
what part

ROTATIONAL GRAVITY

for those I know
and love
those I don't too
adrift on waves in
storm approaching ocean
not in a boat ... only in my swim suit
rolling ... being afloat ... sky falls
left right ... behind n in front
walking back sand beach
impressed by how
I feel some times in gravity
is
so different in water
or
in love

WHO

am I
to endeavor to
inform or enlighten
any one
pompous pronounce preach
or confuse
I am here to amuse
n
delight ... twist a word
brake a line ...
wink ... giggle ... flirt ... n
run down the hall
laughing

YOU KNOW

I am gonna say this
about some both science sixpence fiction
n assorted drone bone wig warn bullshit
that seems (zombie apocalyptic auditorium)
music fade to ... three bicycles n soft piano key
strokes
in my wild days ... l had very little imagination
only poor impulse control ... drugs crime ... loud
motorcycle ... restless brain syndrome
now
in my dotage contemplative stage
pretty sure there is a whole lot
of shaking goin on ... in labs both
above n below board ... a tear full homage
to Gene Wilder ... n young frnnnunnnsteeeeennn
% of brain functions ... resistance to data
doctored intel ... that is not very intelligence
no how ... l have seen time of plenty
a few bad years ... but never went hungry
now
not living in anger fear resentment or despondency
my only concern
is to die alone ... left to wonder
at
how this whole drama called *the world*
ends

MY

pal jack
just called one
of the *political operatives*
a
"shit bonbon"
that I think for me
says more
than every #watdafktag
ever

sort of amusing to me *its going down* burn this
burn that ... face off stand up ... push back ... an
not a one of these major revolutionaries have ever
heard the sound of a sucking chest wound ... or the
splat bullets make hitting flesh

SPACE SUIT

or bubble helmet
some shit
simple as being in
a stupid market
watching some *large* woman
snarling at check stand
over some giant bag of processed garbage
over either price or size
not hearing but seeing
a twisted rage face ... what has happened\
what is happening to this country
she walks out the store ... still muttering
n her
car has a TRUMP sicker
n a confederate flag plate frame
o
boy ... nother day in Florida

A GIFT OF GRIEF

Ah boyo.s gwan
wit all that
(melancholic assuming ... pocket full of bad marbles)
sally nice tits
n barry beer boy who worked at
acme bomb works
or integrated rifle factory ... installing rock+roll
switches
are
as guilty as we are
of *spreading freedom and justice n liberty
for all ... in the name of Jesus n
mom's store bought
apple pie*
consider stocks n bonds ... *some time ya win*
some time ya lose ... even we
got dem blues
fuck it ... it would be really funny
if it had
not gone on ... for 46 more years
same salt content in tears
from ho an to aleppo

CELL PHONE ANOMALOUS

not autonomous or anonymous
cause no body talks to ya
any
way
so busy scrolling ... texting
an
calling each other names
the Television future right
in your hand
Chester Gould ... had Dick Tracy
doing that
before any of the wizz kids
now
were born

CONSTITUTE

novels ... stories ... essay ... proclamations of
love forever or some shit
boring detail ... and *plot*
some body get the butter
or
who got who in what
kind of jackpot
why? says poetry bother
when
all ya gotta do is
be brief
be brilliant
be gone

KRYTRIOLIAN PARALAXUS

as in
eye doctor ... therapist ... dentist
n lawyer
banker ... post office workers ... super market
check stand bandits
assorted *clients* whose reels resemble
under sea urchins
given that ... a long ago life
of crime debauchery self destructive lack
of impulse control
a to this day problem with dates times places
fuzzy recollections of *citizenship*
meaning I do care
snap chat ... counter top ... insta fame flame blame
game
all suddenly inhabit my cross eye ... side sight
n of all the damn things a full grown
coral snake (deadly motherfucker if there is one)
just slithered across my back yard
so pretty ... like a gag me bag of dope
or a bottle of green death
ya never know do ya?

ONE YELLOW

one black
butterfly circle
morning glory flowers
only to convince
me
I do in deed
give a fuck

CULTURAL APPROPRIATION

fuck yu
yr PC gone over too
as if
nine guys who made millions
on *singing the blues*
while Lightnin Hopkins died poor
n
all the rest of the dread lock
hippies
were just being cool ... all of this current
social up roar ... is a bunch of pick n choose
who
ya wanna hear from??? death row
or some high priced condo
in SF or NY
n mean while
my buddy the greatest conga drummer ever
lives on 800 bucks a month
fuck all you all spoiled rich kids
I shudda stole yr lunch
money back when I could still
run fast

MY BUDDY

posted a word ... *malapropism*
last few days
all I can figure
is
things have always been either
giddy
or
shitty
depending on
yr
pantry
mood
surroundings
HOWEVER
when "the best minds of my generation"
are
busy ... building new bombs ... guns ... means
of delivering
death
I gotta go with *shitty*
ya don't smell it see it taste it walk in it
ya
assume (o dear) ats a way it is
n
waddya gonna do
bout it ... (emoji es lack *diversity*)
another crack I heard
last crop of tomatoes come to
papa
n get made into sauce
tears in Florida ... very not giddy

PROGRESS

I guess
SRO skid row hotels
now
gutted n turned into (ready)
luxury condos ... designed by percypuce n
wackanoodle
starting at 2.4 million
come
see the experience you dreamed about
as
I wonder how they got the
thunder bird smell out
the halls ... back then when SOHO
was home to ... (some rather interesting fellas)
Wait ... new occupancy with special 421a tax codes
and ya wanna know
why
I don't

QUENNUS PERSONUS DRAMATUS

my entire whine snivel tremble shake
over the dentist
I should be slapped
what a fkn baby
I had way more pain n suffering
pulling a hook outta my hand
the other morning ... the dentist
felt like a caress I been bit harder by bugs
my usual joke OK
hey doc you know how to tell if a Italian is gay?
Doc Massagllia ... says
"you really wanna ask me that when I got
a drill in my hand"
all in all pretty cool
4 more visits I gonna look
like Cary Grant
(and long as he been dead ... I might pull that off)

A FEW QUESTONS

who is Harley Quinn
what is a bitmogi
who has the answer to "who am I"
"why are we here"
is there a good reason for fire ants
Did Johnny Mathis make a deal w/ Faust
have you seen my little red rooster
does any thing beside kids and dogs make sense
other wise
next *have a nice day*
crack
at me
I gonna puke on yr shoes

ON

an empty Oklahoma
road
I watched America
lose any
an all respect
it ever if ever
deserved or had
an if you come to me
with blue lives matter
after ... that ... you better be
wearing your Make America Great Again
hat
so I
have some thing
to
aim
at

THE WAY

some bugs n snakes
use bright colors to
warn they are *toxic*
I wish whats her name
would
have
worn glow in the dark
underwear

JUST FOR ME

I would love
to know
where how so many
toy soldiers
can afford
to play ... "patriot" (read peace full protest)
do
they not
have to work?
are some nebulous "finance" daddies
involved
for one minute forget history
of stolen land ... who got over on who ... then ... no
think NOW
we have been
about 70 years now
on
a path of violence war depredation of any
"values"
unless ... your "club members"
dry sage brush arid land
is not "insured"
so
some body is pay somebody
to act
out this land of the free bullshit
till
a bill of blood or that blind bitch
Justice is served ... as in a few cases

of late ... watch
Middle East disintegrate ... world markets
go belly up
n
my only comfort is
I know how cold it is in East Oregon

MANGIA MIA

ale iron skillet
no fail me now
chopped onion n peppers
green salsa n garlic
shrimp n spinach
in Mama Caspadora's olive oil
pot o rice
n sittin on da
deck
on Alfred E Newman's not birth day
what
me
worry?
nope

2:08 AM

blasted awake
by dreams
sitting still
breathing ... trying
to answer (to my self questions of "culture")
like
was Doris Day
a rage bitch
in real life
or
is Lady Ga Ga
a nice
Italian girl
who can cook
Zombies ... women who call make up
war paint
n
this problem of
being old enough to
have seen vast changes
in acceptable behavior
on and off screen

AMOMO BAMMO

any way
this guy up near Yakama
has this fish farm
n got a big cash pay out
from some "investor" ok
so he goes n sees
double down back town
Louie (I got it all) Cabezziaa
n buys a half k of blow
n three bags of annex my blues pills ... right
so one night
fried to his eyeballs
he hears noises ... n ... flashing lights
so he tosses his whole stash
ka splash
da fish know not
to fight fuck or go blind
any way ... comes to a day or so later
n figures well ... better be more careful ... OK
n dip nets a truck load of
loaded salmon
to market to market with pinned eyeballs
n twitching fins
any way
every body who eats em
has mixed "feelings"
I only seek to amuse

LASTLY

some Belladonna dream
in a linear collider atoms n protons
assembled by morons
in search of either science
or magic
ray bounce in vivid neon color
n
mice ... watch ... from a mouse hole
n
crack up ... "its the cheese stupid"

the Priest was quicker on the draw
I wound up a praying in consort with Orthodox
monks
who made the toughest guy in Folsom look dainty
(inner strength wise)
now the one real advantage of
older slower harder of hearing
I know that back hat wearing
smooth talkin demon is still
wondering where the fuck is Nic Nac
but I can not hear its murmur
or run fast enough to catch up
as he sells that powder by the boat load
ahh my kayak is my only real
rebellion or finger raise to the
noise n shadows
yet the green water
has a few dark spots, kind of out of focus sirens call
I avoid em
maybe I can not run any more
but
I can paddle my ass off

SILENT SORROWS

door way suffused light
leading
up a flight
of carpet stairs
a face chase
place
she looked out
an up stairs
window saw
him drive by
waved a ring less fingered hand
objects in mirror are closer than they appear
echo bounce sad love song
sung
in discord harmony
off key
each note choke
breathing thru tears
oblivion hi way
always
yesterday

REQUIEM

for Hitch Bot
was
the world not ready to face new ideas?
was
it just yr run of the mill
vandal?
Philly ... has a few of those
n
some anger too

given tech blog ... news feed
talk of robotic interaction
some one
might have been resentful
of a brave new world
in deed

then local drama
ok
land crabs ... big blue ones
small red ones ... invaded my garage

bout 13 of em

now ... they will bite yr fuckin finger if ya let em
but a
bait net and quick
hands
over the fence they go

I calls Joey ... you ever seen land crabs here
he grew up in this house
yep he says ... wait till the big rain comes
they will be every where
close the garage door you
old blind deaf dummy ... chuckle

but Hitch Bot ... who was not nocturnal
and needed human help to
get from place to place
met a spare parts spew end

some how not killing crabs
they are some ugly bastards
might ... in my own silly dilly lavender blue
brain
balance it out

poor hitch bot ... beeeep

A BIT

frightening en lighting moody melodramatic
like a movie
not a dream
some many room apt ... in
a city I have never been in
with a few repairs needed
(I know the cars came from Velvet fan page)
a Simca and a big round Buick both
red n white
a woman with lots of clothes
on ... like a layered look ... but in n out of focus
no idea how I got there who she was
why I was dreaming it ... as I was dreaming it
I kept trying to figure out the triggers
reference points ... but none of the objects
or furniture as familiar as it seemed
had ever been part of my life ... even recall some
wonderful old wood kitchen pieces in frisco
no
this was strange again scary but I was
not
scared
a few times we looked at each other
as she asked me to fix this or that
adjust the window ... tighten up a vent
get the car started pull this extra
stuff to the curb ... one woven chair was a lion
one was this I am sure some design fawn over
dead in New York upper east side kind of
period thing or another
any way
she makes some tea n crumpets
(I know laugh me n tea n crumpets)
any way I see this Icon on the wall

and all of a sudden dream fold open to
like some Elvira Madigan or some other
sappy love movie
an I really see her face
"can it be you?" I say, 'tis me has been
since I was sold ... and abused
after you left me 49 years ago
no no no
(not a bit of this ever happened in my life
but in this drama dream scape it was real as death
or taxes)
"we were to be married ... you went off to war ...
it was cruel for a year but some man bought me
and left me all this pile of dead memory walls"
she knew some people I know n I knew some
ones she did ... then it turns sort of Fellini n we
go to this woman priest who is a carnival barker
n high roller of tarot card n lace face place of
spend money get predicted or really get evicted
who knows
I woke up ... lie there ... what the fuck was that
a complication explanation reflecting on
I went to war a fresh face fat boy ... who loved
poems
n the idea of love
came back a thousand yard stare
this
dream
was why when who what was
some kind of dump out a give a fuck not basket
n move on
waking up at 2:53 on face book
proves it was frightening and enlightening

SUPPOSE

in my brain's closet
hang like a shirt
not worn for years
some
event memory passing thru
a pocket ... n ya move a hanger
n feel it
like a lump
bump
bit of movie ticket nostalgia
gears mesh ... clutch disengage
n
cramba ... yr back in
some place ya have not
been
forever
like a week or so ago
or
in yr cradle ... plotting escape
to
toy land

NO WORD PUBLIC

today
sadness took
my voice
away

Dominic Albanese has been dubbed the *spartan, colloquial poet of a generation*. He fishes on Florida's Treasure Coast, where he has an uneasy truce with fire ants.

END SPOT

Gary McFarland
80 miles an hour
thru beer can country
El Topo
Mid night dream shows
neon cafe, windows
"sad eyed lady of the lowlands"
I am
my poems are
as we all are
a product of our times
the works of some Poets and Jugglers
I have been fortunate enough to know
read with and admire
all part of this life...we live love and
share
Linda Post, I loved you the minute I met you
and you are gone now
but you are the juggler
of a lot my dreams

CPSIA information can be obtained
at www.ICGtesting.com
Printed in the USA
LVHW091936300621
691401LV00002B/85

9 781950 433216